300

Incredible Things for Beanie Lovers on the Internet

VIP Publishing
Marietta, Georgia • (800) 909-6505
Distributed by M.K. Distributors, Inc.

ISBN 0-9658668-5-8

Introduction

When I started this book, I was chatting with a friend who commented that his daughter became interested in the Internet because she loved Beanies. My original plan had not really focused on encouraging "unconnected" people to go online to pursue their passion. However, the Beanie world has proven to me that the Internet can enhance just about any hobby or interest. I have also found that this book helps kids, adults, teachers and parents become more familiar with the vast resources of the Internet. I hope you enjoy this book as much as I have in writing it.

Ken Leebow
Leebow@News-letter.com
http://this.is/TheLeebowLetter

About the Author

Ken Leebow has been in the computer business for over 20 years. The Internet has fascinated him since he began exploring its riches a few years ago, and he has helped thousands of individuals and businesses understand and utilize its resources.

When not on the Net, you can find Ken playing tennis, running, reading or spending time with his family. He is living proof that being addicted to the Net doesn't mean giving up on the other pleasures of life.

— Dedication —

To the kid in all of us, especially my kids, Josh and Alissa.

Acknowledgments

Putting a book together requires many expressions of appreciation. I do this with great joy, as there are several people who have played vital roles in the process:

- My kids, Alissa and Josh, who helped identify some of the cool sites.

- My wife, Denice, who has been patient with me while I have spent untold hours on the Internet.

- Paul Joffe and Janet Bolton, of *TBI Creative Services*, for their editing and graphics skills and for keeping me focused.

- The multitude of great people who have encouraged and assisted me via e-mail.

- Mark Krasner and Janice Caselli for sharing my vision of the book and helping make it a reality.

Books by Ken Leebow

300 Incredible Things to Do on the Internet

300 Incredible Things for Kids on the Internet

300 Incredible Things for Sports Fans on the Internet

300 Incredible Things for Golfers on the Internet

300 Incredible Things for Beanie Lovers on the Internet

America Online Web Site Directory
Where to Go for What You Need

TABLE OF CONTENTS

TABLE OF CONTENTS (continued)

CHAPTER I
CREAM OF THE BEAN CROP

1
Beanie Babies

http://www.ty.com
If you haven't been to the official Ty site, this is a great place to start. Over 2.5 billion hits have already been counted.

2
Keep in Touch

http://www.tcjj.com/beaniecontact.html
One problem on the Net is that companies often fail to provide detailed corporate contact information at their official Web sites. Go here to find out exactly how to write, call, fax or e-mail the folks at Ty.

3

I'm Current
http://www.ty.com/beanie/list/current.html
Here are the current Beanie Babies.

4

I'm Retired
http://www.ty.com/beanie/list/retired.html
These are the ones that have been retired from production.

5

Sort It Out

http://www.bejeanie.com/goodies/sortbirthdaypage1.html
http://www.bejeanie.com/goodies/sortcategorypage1.html
http://www.bejeanie.com/goodies/sortgenderpage1.html
http://www.bejeanie.com/goodies/sortintrodatepage1.html
http://www.bejeanie.com/goodies/sortretiredpage1.html
http://www.bejeanie.com/goodies/sortstylepage1.html
Arrange and view all Beanie Babies by: birthday, category, gender, introduction date, retirement date or style number.

6

Take Me to Ty.com

http://www.beanie-buddy.com/tysites.html
You can get to Ty's official site by way of several subdomains. This site lists many of them.

7
They Mean Business

http://www.beaniebiz.com
This site calls itself "the most comprehensive resource for Beanie Babies collectors on the Internet."

8
Fraud Alert

http://www.beaniemom.com/fakes.html
http://www.erols.com/rklion/fraud.html
Make sure you buy the real thing. This site informs you about fake Beanies.

9
Happy Birthday

http://www.jwp.bc.ca/saulm/bb.htm
Here's a really cool and sophisticated Beanie birthday calendar.

10
Take the Course

http://www.beanies101.com
This site introduces you to the world of Beanies and includes questions
frequently asked by collectors.

11
Wild, Wild, Beanies

http://www.wildaboutbeanies.com
If you're reading this book, then I'm sure you are indeed wild about them. This site
has everything you need to know.

12
Just the FAQs

http://www.bejeanie.com/faq.htm
http://www.netlabs.net/hp/friendly/beanfaq.htm
Even more than you ever needed to know about Beanies.

13
Beanie History 101
http://www.thebeanpatch.com/history.htm

http://www.geocities.com/~beaniemonium/history.html

If you love Beanies, then you should know a little about their beginnings.

14
The Front Nine
http://www.a2zbeaniebabies.co.uk/features/original9.htm

Speaking of history, here are the first nine Beanie Babies. When were they introduced? The answer is January 8, 1994.

15
Picture This
http://www.beaniebid.com/current.htm

http://www.beaniebid.com/retired.htm

http://www.beaniebid.com/pillow.htm

http://www.beaniebid.com/buddy.htm

Great pictures of all your buds.

16
My Check List
http://www.beanie-buddy.com/checklst.html
http://www.addictedtobeaniebabies.com/list.htm
http://members.tripod.com/~BeaniesPage/checklist.html
http://www.geocities.com/EnchantedForest/Dell/5035/bblist.html
If you're a collector, you gotta have a checklist. Here are a few for you.

17
Where's Your Checklist?
http://www.gshirts.com/gshirt/bbtz.html
Do you frequently misplace your Beanie checklist? Order a checklist on a T-shirt and wear it everywhere.

18
Your Friend Indeed
http://www.tcjj.com/beaniebuddy.html
This is one buddy's site you will want to visit frequently. Hang out awhile with your friends.

19
Card Tracker

http://www.mindspring.com/~mrevie/misc/tclist.html
Are you a Beanie card collector? Here's a checklist for your card collection.

20
Track Your Beans

http://www.beanlist.com
Be a bean counter and track your Beanies online.

21
My Price Guide

http://www.beaniex.com/publist0.html
http://www.beanieland.com/guide.html
http://www.beaniemom.com/beanprimar53.html
http://www.beanieworld.net/value/price.html
Here are a few sites that will give you a good idea about the current prices of Beanies. Do you have one worth $5,000?

22
More Price Guides
http://home.att.net/~rascalz/prices.html
http://members.aol.com/Beans45014/Price-Guide.html
http://members.tripod.com/~TEXAS1/BEANIE-PRICE-GUIDE3-index.html
Print out a price guide and use it to help with your inventory.

23
What's That Beanie Cost?
http://compare.beaniebiz.com
This site allows you to look up a Beanie Baby and find out its value.

24
Encyclopedia of Beanies
http://www.encyclobeaniea.com
Yes, there is an encyclopedia dedicated to Beanies. It's a printed book, but there are also lots of interesting things at the site.

25
File This One
http://www.beaniephiles.com
You'll find a Beanie glossary, biographies and much more at Beaniephiles.

26
The Stats Page
http://www.geocities.com/EnchantedForest/Glade/1500/beaniestats.html
The Beanies, the poems, birthdays and more.

27
Beanie Land
http://www.beanieland.com
You've landed in the right spot. Rumors, contests, chats and more are at this site.

28
<u>Beanie Express</u>
http://www.beanie-express.com
Great listing of all Beanies…from rare to Teenies, it's all here.

29
<u>The Message is Out</u>
http://www.bejeanie.com
This site bills itself as "your door to hundreds of pages of Beanie Babies news and information and the award-winning software for Beanie Babies collectors and more!"

30
<u>Mother's Unite!</u>
http://www.momsunited.com
These sweet moms say, "Come for the Beanies, Stay for the Friendships!"

31
It's Phenomenal

http://www.beaniephenomenon.com
That might be an exaggeration, but the graphics are great (check out the e-mail icon). The ladies who operate this site offer a Beanie authenticity service, a Beanie history and more.

32
Beanie Repair

http://www.crosslink.net/~gwvenia
Got a Beanie in need of a little fixin'? The Beanie Hospital is for your emergencies.

33
Tell Me Why

http://apps3.vantagenet.com/zpolls/count.asp?id=9130193016
In this very unscientific poll, find out why people collect Beanies.

34
Funky Momma
http://www.funkymommy.com
This mom has tons of good stuff at her site.

35
Counterfeit
http://www.crittersbbsuperstore.com/counterfeit2.htm
Say it isn't so! Would someone actually create counterfeit Beanies?

CHAPTER II
READ ALL ABOUT IT

36
Ty Warner
http://www.forbes.com/forbes/102196/5810276a.htm
No doubt, Ty Warner is a successful businessman. Let Forbes tell you about the genius behind Beanies.

37
The Real Thing
http://www.realbeanies.com
Hard news reporting about Beanies at this site.

38
All Things Considered
http://www.npr.org/ramfiles/980428.atc.06.ram
National Public Radio has an 8-minute RealAudio spot about Beanie Babies. If you have the RealAudio plug-in, listen away. RealAudio is available at www.realaudio.com.

39
Beanies in the News
http://www.thebeanpatch.com/news.htm
Beanies seem to appear in the news frequently. Read all about them here.

40
Beanie Times
http://www.bhome.com/times.htm
This site has "All the Beanie news that's fit to print."

41
Current News
http://members.xoom.com/lovebeanies/beaniebullbd.html
Here's late breaking news that is updated daily.

"I jumped over the moon, for pete sake!
I should be swamped with endorsement offers,
but all I got was a stupid nursery rhyme!
You're a lousy agent, Bernie!"

42
Beanie Mania
http://www.beaniemania.com
Stores, tips, auctions and fun stuff can be found here.

43
More Beanie Mania
http://www.beaniemania.net
This is the Web site for the magazine of the same name.

44
Beans!
http://www.beansmagazine.com
Bean Magazine wants to help you stay current with all of your collecting needs. This site has a price guide, mall, feature articles and a place to win prizes.

45
Mom Knows Best

http://www.beaniemom.com
The Beanie Mom Netletter is dedicated to Beanie lovers around the world who enjoy reading and learning about Beanies. Lots of great stuff; check out the price list.

46
It's a Bear's World

http://www.bearworld.com
If you love Teddy Bears, why not hibernate here for a couple of years?

47
Beanie World

AOL Keyword Beanieworld
http://www.beanieworld.net
Get all your Beanie news from this award-winning magazine.

48
For Kids Only
http://www.beanieworldkids.com
Mary Beth has a spot just for kids. There's a big list of all the Beanies and lots of other fun stuff, too.

49
Value Guide
http://www.collectorbee.com/beanie.html
Buy a value guide or get news, rumors, chat and more at this site.

50
Beanieholics
http://www.geocities.com/Heartland/Park/4116
Get your Beanie news from around the Internet at this site. You'll get rumors, information, clipart and more.

51
Beanie Collectors
http://www.hotcoco.com/counter/beanies/special/beaniebios.htm
Meet a few Beanie collectors, and read their brief Beanie stories.

52
Beanie News
http://www.beanie411.com/news.html
Cuddle up to the screen and read about your favorite subject.

53
Eagle Eyes
http://www.wichitaeagle.com/extras/beanies/index.htm
The Wichita Eagle has a site dedicated to Beanies. Lots of information and news at this site.

54
Chicago Sun Times
http://www.suntimes.com/index/beanie.html
This major newspaper has weekly articles about your Beanie friends.

55
Rumors R Us
http://www.tcjj.com/beanierumor.html
http://www.beaniekeepers.com/rumors.html
http://members.aol.com/beans45014/news.html
http://www.beaniesandbears.com/RumorArchive.htm
We all love a few good rumors. Here are some about Beanies.

56
What's the Count?
http://comm1.digits.com/wc?—info=yes&—name=bongo
Ty's official site has recorded billions of visits. This site tells you even more detailed statistics about how many hits Ty.com is getting.

57
Be Happy
http://www.happytoy.com
Everything you ever needed to know about Teenie Beanies and other McDonald's Happy Meal Toys.

58
The Sporting Life
http://www.beaniemadness.com/sports.html
Which sports teams have given away Beanies? Find out here.

59
Showtime
http://www.beansmagazine.com/info/calendar.html
Find out where and when the Beanie shows will be held, and get together with other fans.

60
Buy the Book

http://www.wildaboutbeanies.com/books.htm
http://www.foryourangels.com/beaniebooks.htm
http://www.funkymommy.com/funky/beaniebooks.htm
There are many books available about Beanies. Here are a few good ones.

CHAPTER III
DON'T FORGET THE FUN

61
A Real Fan(atic)
http://www.thebeanpatch.com/closehomecomic.gif
I searched high and low for some funny Beanie cartoons. Here's one that should bring a smile to your face.

62
Help, I'm a Beaniac!
http://www.pldi.net/~cagles/okiebeans1.htm
You might be a beaniac if…

63
Ty's Games
http://www.ty.com/beanie/games
Ty has some fun games for you: jigsaw puzzles, crossword puzzles, calendars and much more.

64
Puzzle Emporium
http://www.cardemporium.com/games.html
While at the emporium, here are a few puzzles to play with.

65
Puzzled?
http://www.beaniebid.com/scripts/puzzle/slidepuzzle.html
Billionaire Bear has been arranged in a very strange way. Here's your opportunity
to put the pieces back together.

66
Slide Over
http://www.nadinesplace.pair.com/puzzle/slider.htm
Shuffle 'em up and then put this puzzle together.

67
Peace Man
http://a2ztoys.com/java/slider2
You might go crazy putting Peace back together.

68
How's Your Memory?
http://www.nadinesplace.pair.com/puzzle/memory.htm
Play this Beanie memory game, and you'll know the answer.

69
Crossword Puzzle
http://www.a2zbeaniebabies.co.uk/crossword/index.htm
Fortunately for all of us, this puzzle is easier to solve than the ones in the New York Times.

70
Win a Beanie
http://www.kidsdomain.com/kids/contests.html
Hey, what could be more fun than winning a Beanie for free?

71
Tails You Win
http://www.beanietales.com/contests.html
Here are a few contests where you can win a Beanie. Good luck.

72
FYI
http://www.pldi.net/~cagles/okiebeans6.htm
For your information, if you send these folks a phrase that forms a Beanie name as an acronym, you might win a Beanie.

**"I spent months trying to pop it—
I thought it was a pimple."**

73
Java Beans
http://members.xoom.com/kkopcha/java.htm
Play a few games "programmed" in Java. Hot stuff!

74
Beanie Fun!
http://www.beaniefun.com
http://www.fairfieldkids.com/beaniecalendar.htm
It really is fun. Print out a calendar with Beanies on it, track your Beanies, play games and more.

75
Talk to Me!
http://www.republicjewelry.com/beanies.htm
Bet you didn't know Beanies can talk. Listen to them here.

76
Greetings, Beanie Buddy
http://www.beanie-buddy.com/postoffice.html
http://www.thebeanpatch.com/postcardshop.htm
Go ahead, send one of your friends a Beanie E-greeting.

77
Teenie Beanie Postcard
http://happytoy.com/cgi-t/postcard
http://dmapub.dma.org/~nielsodc/beanie
If you prefer "mailing" Teenie Beanies, here's your site!

78
Billy Bear's Playground
http://billybear4kids.com/beanie/babies.htm
It would take an entire book to describe all the fun and interesting things at Billy Bear's site. Do yourself a favor, and go there right now! Billy's waiting.

79
Enter the FunZone
http://www.fairfieldkids.com/beaniefunzone.htm
This site is packed with cool things to print out like calendars, bookmarks, checklists, stationery and thank you cards.

80
Stationery.com
http://www.angelfire.com/me/beaniepizazze/stationery.html
Print out your own stationery with your favorite Beanie on it.

81
I'm a Poet
http://www.tcjj.com/beaniepoem.html
http://members.aol.com/ebeanies/poems.htm
http://www.angelfire.com/tn/RJBeanieBabies/index.html
http://www.geocities.com/EnchantedForest/Cottage/8799/Poem.html
We all know Beanies come with poems. Here are many for you.

82
Happy Birthday
http://www.beanies4you.com/beanie_babie_birthdays.htm
Check out all the Beanies' birthdays. Beanies4You also has a rumors section, and
they will be happy to sell you some Beanies.

83
What's Your Sign?
http://www.beckettassociates.com/beckett/zodiac.asp
You know their birthdays, but do you know about their astrological signs?

84
Beanie Poll
http://www.octane.com/beaniebasher/poll.html
What do you think should happen to Beanies? Take this poll and see what other
folks say.

85
Your Beanie Booklet
http://www.geocities.com/EnchantedForest/Glade/9094/beaniefun.html
Print out this Web site and you'll have a fun booklet with a word search, name
that Beanie, Beanie coloring pages and many more fun things to do.

86
Poll Vault
http://www.freevote.com/booth/beaniejungle
Who's your favorite Beanie? Vote here.

87
Beanie Trivia
http://catalog.com/beanies/btc
http://www.momsunited.com/trivia.html
How much do you know about Beanies? Test your knowledge here.

88
More Beanie Trivia

http://catalog.com/beanies/btc
http://www.thebeanpatch.com/trivia.htm
Can't get enough trivia? Here are a few more sites for you.

89
Even More Beanie Trivia

http://www.republicjewelry.com/bbtriv2.htm
http://www.wichitaeagle.com/extras/beanies/basics/trivia.htm
"The American flag I wear with pride, my long trunk I just can't hide. Who am I?"
Find lots of questions (and answers) at this site.

90
Take the Quiz

http://www.republicjewelry.com/Beaniemc.htm
http://www.geocities.com/~2muchty4u/quiz.htm
Okay, so you don't like multiple choice tests, but you'll probably ace these.

91
Beanie Babies Running Wild
http://homearts.com/depts/home/87beanf1.htm
This very well designed site has trivia questions and the history of Ty
and Beanies.

92
Ask the Wizard
http://www.thebeanpatch.com/BeanieWizard.htm
Got a Beanie question? Ask the Wizard. You will be sure to get an answer.

93
Put the Puzzle Together
http://members.tripod.com/~ChillyBeans/puzzle/puzzle.htm
A fun puzzle game for you. Pick your Beanie.

94
Tic Tac Toe
http://members.tripod.com/~ChillyBeans/nc/ncross.htm
Forget the X's and O's. We're gonna play with Beanies. This simple game is a lot of fun.

95
Hang Man
http://members.tripod.com/~ChillyBeans/hang/hang.htm
An old-time favorite goes high-tech.

96
Just Beans
http://www.kidskourt.com/Themes/JustBeans.htm
Play some Beanie games, and enjoy some of the desktop themes.

97
Beanie Quiz
http://www.awesomebeanies.com/bbquiz.html
Take a quiz. There's one for newbies and another for experts.

98
GI Joe?
http://www.brunching.com/toys/toy-beanieorjoe.html
What do GI Joe and Beanie Babies have in common? Here's a clue: What's in a name?

99
Beanie Mad Libs
http://members.xoom.com/kkopcha/madlibs.htm
Remember Mad Libs? Here's a site that has some designed for Beanies.

100
Game Time
http://www.beaniecottage.com/game.html
How many times can you find Peace's nose in 30 seconds? You'll never know if you don't go to this site.

101
Beanie Desktops
http://www.kidskourt.com/Themes/BeanThemes.htm
Would you like a creative desktop on your computer? In seconds, you can download a great one.

102
Beanie Download
http://www.splashweb.com/beanies/fun_downloads.html
Screensavers, icons and more can be downloaded here.

103
Name That Beanie
http://www.tnpsc.com/ssaver/beanie.htm
A great screensaver that you can download for free.

104
Beanie Lover
http://www2.bluemountain.com/eng/screensaver/SAVheart.html
Here's a screensaver that features hearts. You can even set up your own tag line, such as: "I Love Beanies."

105
Beanie Wallpaper
http://www.fairfieldkids.com/beaniebabywallpaper.htm
Lot's of different wallpapers for you to choose from.

106
Beanie Greetings

http://www.beaniebaby.net/gram
http://www.beaniemania.com/greet/greet.html
http://www.splashweb.com/beanies/sendcard.html
http://www.beaniefun.com/games/postcards/sendcard.cfm
Send a friend or loved one a Beanie greeting. You can also buy Beanies and explore other goodies here.

107
A Beanie Thank You

http://www.fairfieldkids.com/beaniebabythankyoustartpage.htm
Create your own Beanie thank you card for a friend or loved one.

108
English Beanie

http://www.beanienewsuk.com
Beanie information straight from England. Using subtle humor, they even have an FABQ (Frequently Asked Beanie Questions) section.

109
101 Fun Things

http://www.ty.com/beanie/games/101things/index.html
Here are 101 fun things to do with your Beanie Babies. My favorite is #48: make paperweights! They look really cute on my desk.

110
A,B,C

http://www.angelfire.com/tn/RJBeanieBabies/Letters.html
Are you teaching someone the ABCs? This might speed up the process.

111
Rock Climbing

http://www.heartguards.com
This is actually a site that sells product, but the first graphic is what's really cool. Watch out for falling rocks.

112
Colorful Bears
http://www.beaniesandbears.com/KidsPlace.htm
Bring your mouse crayons with you and color away.

113
A Beanie Cruise
http://www.2beannies.com
Yes, take a cruise with all of your Beanie fan friends.

"I'm a rattlesnake and this is my little brother. He's a tattlesnake."

CHAPTER IV
READY TO ORDER

114
Hallmark Knows Beanies
http://www.hallmarkcollectibles.com/tybeanie.htm
Hallmark has tons of Beanies for you.

115
Hallmark Stores
http://www.collectibility.com/halllink.html
Here's a list of many Hallmark stores…on the Net.

116
Shop 'Til You Drop
http://www.beaniebiz.com/online.phtml
This is a list of places on the Net that will sell you Beanies.

117
Stores, Stores, Stores

http://www.jcn1.com/spindler/beanies
http://www.wildaboutbeanies.com/stores.htm
Explore more than 16,000 places to buy Beanies.

118
Buy the List

http://www.listmakers.com
Here's a list of all the stores who sell Beanies. You can purchase this list for a nominal fee.

119
Where's That Store?

http://www.zip2.com
Are you one of those folks who calls all the stores to find a certain Beanie? Use this site to find stores near you that sell Beanies and other collectibles.

120
On the Beat

http://www.beaniepatrol.com
Beanie Patrol is a source for finding retail stores that sell Beanie Babies at
reasonable retail prices.

121
Gift Baskets

http://www.beaniesinabox.com
Thanks for the great gift! Give a gift of Beanies in a basket.

122
Wall to Wall Beanies

http://www.wallos.com
This site claims to be "the world's largest collectibles store." It is well done and
easy to use.

123
Cute Critters
http://www.crittersbbsuperstore.com
This one says, "Relax, you are at Critters, the Internet superstore for Beanie Babies. You won't find any long lines. We have 'em all! So get ready and go find that Beanie you have been looking for!"

124
Beanie Emporium
http://www.cardemporium.com
Here's what they say here: 'Beanie Babies are huge, and we have one of the largest selections available anywhere!" Make a visit to see if they're right.

125
CToys
http://www.ctoys.com
CToys provides information on where to find Beanie Babies, Beanie accessories and other collectible toys.

126
Beanies for Less

http://www.beaniesforless.com
Sounds too good to be true. See if they have a deal for you.

127
What a Bargain!

http://www.bargainbeanies.com
Try to get a bargain on your Beanies.

128
Beanies and Bears

http://www.beaniesandbears.com
Nice graphics, a simple site and a place to buy a lot of Beanies and bears. I guess that's how they came up with the name.

129
E-Beanies

http://www.etail.com/beanies
E-tail sells Beanies online and has a simple Web site which has all the
Beanies—current and retired—with their prices.

130
Etoys.com

http://www.etoys.com
This store is sure to have Beanies for you. And the *good news* is you won't have to
wait in line during the holiday season.

131
Beckett Babies

http://www.beckettassociates.com
Beckett has babies. It's easy to point and click to view them.

132
Take it to the Max

http://www.beaniemax.com
BeanieMax has tons of Beanies and is a well-organized shopping site.

133
Attitude Bears

http://www.ssnd.com
Stone Cold and friends are at this site. Of course, you can buy all the other Beanies, too.

134
Rare Commodities

http://www.republicjewelry.com/repwebbb.htm
Republic Jewelry might have found that there is more money in Beanies than diamonds.

135
Make the Connection
http://www.beanieconnection.com
Here's a fancy site where you can purchase your Beanies.

136
Fribbles Says…
http://www.fribblesandquirks.com
"If it's hot…it's here! Retirements! Exclusives! Newest Additions! We feature inside scoops, exciting announcements and that hard to find stuff!"

137
Beanie World
http://www.beaniebabyworld.com
Buy items here, but I like the rumors, birthdays and—best of all—an arcade. Go play a game or two.

138
<u>Beanie Heaven</u>
http://www.beaniebabyheaven.com
With over 15,000 Beanies in stock, this sounds like heaven to me.

139
<u>A to Z From the UK</u>
http://www.a2zbeaniebabies.co.uk
From England, a great looking Web site with lots of good stuff. And if you want to buy a few Beanies, they'll be happy to sell them to you.

140
<u>Beanie Lady</u>
http://www.beanielady.com
This great lady has created a beautiful site. And she would like you to buy some Beanies here.

141
Collecting Beanies for Fun and Profit

http://www.reel.com/Content/moviepage.asp?mmid=44166

Here's a video Beanie Baby guide that offers investment advice from enthusiasts and information about retired Beanies, variations, and the secondary market. Sure to please and enlighten fans of the popular cuddly collectibles.

142
Take Me to the Patch

http://www.thebeanpatch.com

Here's one of the best-designed Beanie sites on the Net. Besides purchasing Beanies, there is a lot of other cool stuff here.

143
It's a Fun House

http://www.beaniefunhouse.com

Of course, any house with Beanies has to be fun. Use this one to purchase your Beanies.

144
Toon In

http://www.beanietoons.com
The site is dedicated to offering mint condition Beanies at affordable prices.

145
Ye Olde Beanie Shoppe

http://www.thebeaniebabyshoppe.com
This store has all the Beanies listed for you—current and retired—with their appropriate prices.

146
Take Me to the Mall

http://www.tellmall.com
This mall sells just one thing: Beanies!

147
Beanie Buyer

http://www.beaniebuyer.com
The purpose of this site is to assist you in buying and/or selling Beanie Babies. It is an online classified ad section.

148
Mickey Collett's Dilemma

http://www.beaniebaby.com
http://www.beaniebaby.com/order/tylawsuit.html
Mickey has a Web site where you can buy Beanies. However, Ty is suing her for the use of the Web site name.

149
Cards 'n More

http://www.beaniefind.com/cardshop
Buy a Beanie card or puzzle.

150
U.K. Beanie

http://www.lemonlaineydesign.com
All the way from England, you can buy or participate in an auction. Even if you're not in a shopping mood, go for a visit. There's interesting stuff here.

151
Card Shop

http://www.sherow.com/cards
Beanie cards are popular. Here are some that you can view or buy.

152
Kinship

http://www.beaniekins.com
Oops, it's just another retail site that sells Beanies, but I really like the name.

153
Who Am I?

http://www.bbnos.com
"Float like a butterfly, sting like a bee, come and see me!"

154
Buyer Beware

http://www.traderlist.com/caution.html
http://www.beaniephiles.com/safetrades.html
You can never be too careful. So, when buying or trading your Beanies, make sure you are cautious.

155
Is it Real?

http://www.beaniephenomenon.com/authenticity.htm
Would you like a service to check your Beanies for authenticity? Here's someone who will.

156
Survey Says

http://www.ty.com/survey.html

Ty wants to know about your retail buying experience. So, take the survey.

**"See how hard and flat my abs are?
You could look just like me if you worked out!"**

CHAPTER V
NOW TAKING BIDS

157
eBay Beanies

http://pages.ebay.com/beaniebabies
Ebay is the major auction site on the Internet. It has a special site dedicated to Beanie Babies.

158
Beanie Nation

http://www.beanienation.com
It's so popular, it has its own nation. Check it out and see a large auction site.

159
Shop 'til You Drop

http://www.myshop.com
Over 12,000 members auction their wares at this site.

160
Beanie Universe
http://www.auctionuniverse.com
Auction away—there are thousands of Beanies available at this site.

161
Yahoo! Beanies
http://auctions.yahoo.com
Yahoo! will not be left out of the auction action.

162
Just Beanies
http://www.justbeanies.com
Here's an auction sited dedicated to just Beanies.

163
Beanie Time
http://www.beanietime.com
It's always Beanie time! Join the auction at this site.

164
It's Mine
http://www.yourbeanieauction.com
Okay, it's yours too. Sign up for free for this auction.

165
Exhange Please
http://www.beaniex.com
You got a Beanie you want to exchange with someone else? This site has traded over 75,000!

166
Exchange My Beanie
http://www.beanieexchange.net

You can exchange Beanies with other people. Find tons of news and information at this site.

167
Collector.net
http://www.worldcollectorsnet.com/beanie

Read the message boards to see if there is a Beanie or discussion topic of interest to you.

168
I'll Bid...
http://www.beaniebid.com

This is a place to buy and sell Beanies, but there are plenty of other things to do here.

169
Baby Dot Net
http://www.beaniebaby.net
Buy, chat, send a card and more at Baby Dot Net.

170
Trading FAQs
http://www.netlabs.net/hp/friendly/tradefaq.htm
If you're trading Beanies on the Net, make sure you have your FAQs straight.

171
Trading.com
http://www.traderspage.com
Bid and trade for your Beanie friends.

172
Trading Places
http://noxorcsoft.simplenet.com/Tradingcards.htm
Are you a Beanie card trader? This place lists a bunch of places to trade them.

173
Trade.com
http://www.traderlist.com
Here's a trading group that you can join.

CHAPTER VI
ACCESSORIES ARE EVERYTHING

174
Track Your Beanies

http://noxorcsoft.simplenet.com
http://www.plushcollector.com
If you're a serious collector, you might want this software. It has a pretty cool tracking screen.

175
Download Please!

http://www.bean-ebuy.com/downloads.shtml
Get a free Beanie Collectors spreadsheet. You can track purchase price, current price, current value of your collection and the difference in cost and current value.

176
Sleep Tight
http://www.stuffedtoydodads.com
Fun and creative ways to store your prized possessions.

177
Beanie Home
http://www.354.com/beaniebabyhomes.htm
Every Beanie needs a roof over its head.

178
Habitat for Beanie
http://www.beaniehabitats.com
If your Beanie doesn't have a home of its own, it can find a habitat right here

179
Mooove...
http://www.beaniebarn.net
... on over to the barn and store your favorite pets in this barn.

180
Beanies on the Bus...
http://www.beanmobiles.com
... go up and down.

181
Camp Beanie
http://www.beaniebunkhouse.com
Now that you have a ton of Beanies, you need to place them in a Cubby Cottage.

182
Rising Tide

http://www.beanieark.com
In the event of a flood, you might want to store your Beanies in an ark.

183
Beanies and the Bean Stalk

http://www.bean-stalk.com
Do you have so many Beanies that you need a "Bean Pole?" This item will hold up to fifty-two Beanies.

184
Go Climb a Tree

http://asisoftware.com/the-tree
Why shouldn't these fun animals hang out in a tree?

185
Cold Climate?
http://www.beaniestuff.com
Do you live in a cold part of the world? If you do, you might want to keep Beanie warm. They have some cool hats and scarves to buy.

186
Put Some Clothes On!
http://www.katieskeepsakes.com/html/clothes/clothes.html
What are you? Some kind of animal? Go here and get some clothes.

187
Do It Yourself
http://craftfinder.com/html/kidpatterns.html
Make clothes for your Beanie friends.

188
Sunbathing
http://www.bestwishes.net/bestwishes/beanbabac.html
Get your beach chairs here. They also sell leashes, fanny packs and backpacks. Be prepared for the next vacation.

189
Diane Does Accessories
http://www.designsbydiane.com/productlist.htm
It looks like these accessories are sold only to stores, but you can get an idea of some nice ones. Check out the glow-in-the-dark sleeping bag.

190
Sit, Beanie, Sit!
http://www.clearlybeanie.com/pedestal.html
If you find that your Beanie doesn't listen to your command, you might want to purchase this accessory.

191
Ty Tags

http://www.beaniex.com/tags.html
http://www.tcjj.com/beanietags.html
http://www.collectibletreasures.net/beaniebabies.htm
Here are all the variations of Ty tags.

192
Tag It!

http://www.tagpreservers.com
If you really love your Beanie, make sure its name tag is preserved.

193
Seeing Rainbows

http://www.rainbowtags.com
A simple page that offers protector tags and Beanie keepers.

"Did you hear? They might make us
wear uniforms to school next year!"

194
Zoo

http://www.productzoo.com
This one refers to itself as, "your one stop online store for Beanie Babies accessories and inflatable furniture."

195
Scenery

http://www.beanie-scenie-group.com
If you have a lot of Beanies, you might want to add these scenery backdrops to your collection.

196
Sittin' on a Park Bench

http://www.republicjewelry.com/beaniecd.htm
Make sure your Beanies get some fresh air. Take them to the park with this bench.

197
Domed Beanies
http://www.deroberts.com/beaniebabie.html
Protect your Beanies with a glass dome.

198
Stop!
http://www.web-weave.com/beanie/bean.htm
Do you brake for Beanies when you see them at roadside stands? Then you better get this bumper sticker.

199
File 'Em Here
http://www.beaniefile.com
If you need an inexpensive way to store your precious friends, check out this filing system.

200
Treasure Chest

http://www.beanie-treasure-chest.com
Get an actual treasure chest to house your precious Beanies.

201
Bag 'Em and Protect 'Em

http://www.beanibags.com
These are bags to protect your Beanies.

202
Fun Stuff

http://www.beaniestuff.com
It says here, "if you love them, leash them!" Don't let those Beanies out of your sight!

203
Accessories Galore
http://www.beanieaccessories.com
Furniture, sweaters and much more are available here.

204
Beanie Stuff
http://www.clever.net/chrisco/beanies/main.htm
Want to buy a Beanie clock, jewelry box, key chain and other stuff? Check it out here.

205
Bear Magnets
http://cornhusker.net/~janf/thebears.html
Not really Beanie magnets, but here are some very nice magnetic bears.

206
Bookmark This
http://www.thelimitedconnection.com/bookmark.html
Get a bean-filled bookmark.

207
Beanie Artist
http://www.beaniemom.com/carlton.html
Carlton Bjork is a very talented artist who has created some excellent artwork.

208
The Beanie Artist
http://www.beanieartist.com
Terrie Sopp Rae has some beautiful artwork for you. Even if you're not in a buying mood, make a visit to see how talented she is.

209
Charming
http://www.angelfire.com/fl/tinythings
These items are indeed charming. Get a Beanie charm or key chain.

210
My Beanie Baby Binder
http://www.mybeaniebabybinder.com
Here's a binder tab book that comes with content and automatic updates. If you're a serious collector and cataloger of Beanies, this might help you get organized.

211
Free Stuff
http://www.ppi-free.com/beanie.html
For free, you can obtain ideas and craft supplies.

212
Beanie Farm
http://www.beaniefarm.com
This farm is not for sale, but it's so cute, I had to include it. See what you think.

213
Beanie T
http://members.home.net/embexpress/beanie.htm
Tell everyone about your love of Beanies by wearing one of these T-shirts.

214
Rhyme Time
http://www.beanierhymes.com
Cards and T's…lots of stuff to please.

CHAPTER VII
FOR THE FANS

215
Ty's Rules
http://www.ty.com/beanie/info/websites.html

Ty has posted a "friendly" legal document that explains policy toward usage of its name, logo and trademarks. If you are creating a Beanie Web page, it would be a good idea to read this document.

216
Law Suits R Us
http://www.planetbeanie.com/lawsuit.htm

If you're going to have a Web site, you don't want to receive one of these letters. Yes, this is an actual letter from Ty's law firm.

217
Surf To…

http://surf.to
There are many fan sites on the Net, and most have very looong Web addresses.
Go here to get a short, simple and free Web address for your site.

218
Surf.to/RealEamples

http://surf.to/beanie
http://welcome.to/beanies
Here are some real examples of simple Web addresses (URLs) that automatically
transfer to the actual, looong addresses.

219
Fly Me To…

http://fly.to/jensbeanworld
… Jeanie's World.

220
Happy Birthday
http://www.angelfire.com/biz2/beaniesparadise/birthday.html
Were any Beanies born on your birthday? Here's a quick way to find out.

221
Be on the Lookout
http://www.geocities.com/EnchantedForest/Dell/6986/geobook.html
Everyone seems to be looking for Beanies. At this site, Beanie fans report where they have seen some.

222
Beanies Anonymous
http://www.addictedtobeaniebabies.com
http://www.addictedtobeaniebabies.com/contest.html
Here's an addicted fan who has decided to tell the world about her addiction.

223
Beanie Fanatic
http://www.beaniemadness.com/test.html
Are you one? Here are 100 questions that will help you determine the answer.

224
Museum
http://www.geocities.com/Heartland/Park/8785/Museum.html
It's a cultural affair at the Beanie museum.

225
Beanie Graphics
http://members.tripod.com/~BeanieHeaven
http://www.listmakers.com/freebies.html
If you have a Beanie Web site, try out these graphics. These folks have been kind enough to create them for your use.

226
More Beanie Graphics
http://www.angelfire.com/me2/beaniepizazze2
http://www.angelfire.com/tn/RosysBeanieBabies/Clipart.html
Got a Web site and a favorite Beanie? You can find some great graphics here.

227
Price Ticker
http://www.splashweb.com/beanies/ticker.html
This one is really cool. For free, place a Beanie Baby price ticker on your Web page.

228
Karissa's Beanies
http://userzweb.lightspeed.net/denney/karissa.html
Karissa is nine years old and has quite a Beanie collection and one heck of a Web site. She admits that her dad helped with the site.

229
Traveling Bear
http://www.geocities.com/Athens/Acropolis/1466
Start out with a bear, then pass it around and see what happens. This sounds like a great project—a lot of fun and learning at the same time.

230
Beanie Cam
http://www.wichitaeagle.com/extras/beanies/beaniecam/front.htm
It's the only Webcam I know that is dedicated to Beanies.

231
Never 2 Much Beanies
http://www.geocities.com/~2muchty4u/main.htm
Learn Beanie vocabulary and find too much other stuff to list. Go for a visit, but make sure you have a lot of time on your hands.

232
Katie and Dad
http://www.geocities.com/EnchantedForest/Glade/2156/index.html
Check out how this family shares its love of Beanies and the Internet.

233
Web Ring Mania
http://www.geocities.com/Heartland/Woods/2218/webring.html
Web Rings take you to different but related sites. In this case, this site lists many Web Rings dedicated to Beanies.

234
Retail Web Ring Mania
http://www.beaniemania.com/ring/ring.html
If you're a retailer, you might want to sign up at this site. If you're a fan, go here and just keep clicking to go to many different Beanie retail sites.

"My therapy is quite simple: I wag my tail and lick your face until you feel good about yourself again."

235
Beanie Crazy
http://members.aol.com/lezly24/menu.html
This "crazed" fan has a simple site that allows you to see all the Beanies and more.

236
Ask Jason
http://www.geocities.com/EnchantedForest/Creek/7404/index.html
Have a question? Jason has the answer.

237
I'd Rather Be In…
http://www.freeyellow.com/members4/shjts/stcroixbeanies.html
… St. Croix, but we'll have to settle for all the latest Beanie news, rumors, gossip and more all in one place.

238
Say It Isn't So!
http://www.octane.com/beaniebasher
This is the Web site that promotes "The Official Beanie Basher Handbook."

239
Pandemonium Over Beanies
http://www.beaniemonium.com
Pen pals, screensavers, news and a lot of other great stuff can be found here.

240
Small Fries
http://www.gate.net/~ronni/teenie98.html
http://www.gate.net/~ronni/teengall.html
http://sarasota.miningco.com/blteenie.htm
These sites have information and pictures about the Teenie Beanies.

241
Promo Only
http://members.aol.com/ebeanies/promotions.htm
Here are details and rumors about future Happy Meal Collectible promotions at McDonald's.

242
Princess
http://www.geocities.com/Heartland/Meadows/5929/index2a.html
Princess, of course, is named after Diana, and here's a great tribute site to her. Ty will be donating profits from this Beanie to the Diana, Princess of Wales Memorial Fund.

CHAPTER VIII
CLUBS AND CHATTING

243
It's Official

http://www.beaniebabyofficialclub.com
Ty has its very own Beanie Baby Club. Go ahead and join the fun.

244
Join the Club

http://www.bbbclub.com
This site says: "We judge you not on how many Beanie Babies you have, but by the happiness you share with your Beanies and others."

245
Want a Pen Pal?

http://www.funkymommy.com/penfriends/penfriends.htm
We all like having friends. See if you can find a pen pal here.

246
Graniacs Unite
http://www.geocities.com/~beaniemonium/graniacs.html
What's a Graniac? It's an older person who loves Beanies and wants a pen pal. So, if you meet those criteria, this site is for you.

247
Collector Cards
http://www.beaniecardclub.com
Here's what this site claims: "With the ability to share information with thousands of members throughout the U.S. and Canada, this is undoubtedly the most comprehensive Web site on the Internet about Beanie Babies Collector's Cards."

248
Original Beanie Babies Club
http://members.aol.com/bongoamy
This is one of the largest and oldest Beanie Babies Clubs on the Internet, with over 7,000 members in the clubhouse.

249
Talk is Cheap
http://www.talkcity.com/chat.htmpl?room=BeanosCentral
TalkCity is one of the major chat sites on the Net. Join in the chatter at
BeanosCentral.

250
Many Bytes Here
http://www.beaniebits.com
Find out about clubs, newsletters, games and even how many Beanie Babies are
on this planet.

251
Can We Chat?
http://beanieshop.com/chat
http://www.myshop.com/boards/beanie
Join a chat group about—what else?—Beanie Babies.

252
Message in a Beanie
http://www.insidetheweb.com/mbs.cgi/mb186355
Tons of questions and answers at this message board.

253
Beanie Newsgroups
http://www.liszt.com
http://www.onelist.com
http://www.egroup.com
Go to these sites, type in "Beanie Babies" and you will be propelled into the world of newsgroups.

254
Deja Beanies
http://www.dejanews.com
Enter "Beanie Babies" in the search box and you can find out who is discussing this popular topic. And of course, you can join the conversation.

255
Club Beanie

http://clubs.yahoo.com/Recreation___Sports/Toys/Beanie_Babies/index.html
Yahoo! has a variety of Beanie clubs for you to join.

CHAPTER IX
FUNDRAISING AND CHARITIES

256
Preemie Charity
http://www.beaniesforpreemies.com
Beanies for Preemies is a nationwide charitable organization dedicated to bringing happiness to premature and critically ill infants.

257
Count Your Blessings
http://www.beanieblessings.com
Here's a book titled: "Beanie Baby Blessings: Stories from the Heart About How Beanie Babies Change Lives." It's always nice to hear a heart-warming story.

258
Infants in Need
http://www.iin.org
This is the place to purchase a Beanie and have the proceeds go to kids in need.

259
Save the Puppies
http://www.beanibags.com/projectbeanie.htm
This Humane Society uses donated Beanies to help raise money to save real animals.

260
Beanie Charity
http://www.toysfortots.com
http://www.toysfortots.com/certificate.html
Purchase a limited edition Beanie Baby and have some of the proceeds go to Toys for Tots.

261
Fund Raisers
http://www.beaniemom.com/fundraisermain.html
Here's a list of fundraising projects you can get involved with or be inspired by.

262
Blackie Visits the World

http://www.iin.org/blackie.htm
This is another heart-warming story about a Beanie and his travels.

263
Halo Forever

http://www.haloforever.com
Don't retire Halo!

CHAPTER X
OTHER BEANIES AND BEARS

264
Disney Knows Beanies

http://www.dizbeanies.com
http://disney.go.com/Shop
"… full of Disney Mini Bean Bag Plush information. So relax, be prepared to spend some time, make some new friends and learn all about Disney's Mini Bean Bag Plush collectibles!"

265
Puffkins

http://www.swibco.com
This is the official site of these cute and cuddly characters.

266
BeanPals

http://www.kellytoy.com
BeanPals and other toys can be found here.

267
Out of This World

http://www.planetplush.com
Hey, these plush characters are kinda cute.

268
Beanie Sports Mascots

http://www.sportsmascots.com
Go ahead, support your alma mater and buy one of these fine Beanies.

269
Meanies

http://www.meanies.com

Have you met Meanies? They're the tough, funny beanbags!

270
Sports Mania

http://www.salvinos.com

Salvinos has sports star bears for you to collect.

271
Sports Heroes and More

http://www.limitedtreasures.com

This site features some of the great sports heroes and other collectible bears.

272
Great Idea

http://www.the-ideafactory.com

Meanies, Spice Girls, Star Trek and more are waiting for you at the Idea Factory.

273
Brainy Babies
http://www.brainybabies.com
Here are some smart ones: Albert Einstein, Ben Franklin, Thomas Edison and many more.

274
Jerry and Friends
http://www.deadbeaniebears.com
Jerry Garcia and some of his bear friends are waiting for you.

275
Warner Brother Beanies
http://www.wbstore.com
What are you waiting for? Bugs Bunny and friends are anxiously awaiting your arrival.

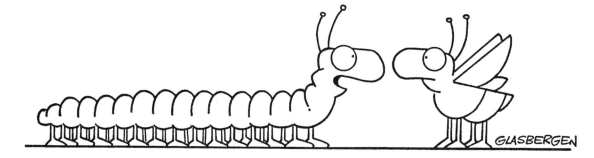

"I tried all the fitness fads, but my doctor was
right all along—walking is still the best exercise."

276
Bugs Only
http://www.bugsbeanies.com
You know that bunny. He's got to have his own Web site.

277
Have a Beanie and Smile
http://www.collectibletreasures.net/toys.htm
Coke, Harley, Kellogg's and other Beanies can be found here.

278
Don't Eat These…
http://www.toyboxc.com/big_kids_stuff/products/index.html
… fruits and vegetables.

279
Feel Good

http://www.bearlycountry.com

Some things in life just make you feel good. Russ Berrie's words will make you feel good, too.

CHAPTER XI
BEANIE LINKS AND SEARCH

280
Not for Kids Only

http://kidscollecting.miningco.com
The Mining Company is also very good at mining information about Beanies on the Net. After all, Beanies are as good as gold.

281
Guide Me

http://www.beaniebabyguide.com
This site is similar to Yahoo!'s directory but is dedicated to Beanie Babies.

282
Excited About Beanies

http://www.excite.com/collectibles
Excite, a major search engine, has auction and classified sections just for Beanie Babies.

283
Top 100

http://www.beanietop100.com
We, the people, vote on which Beanie sites are the best. See what the winners are.

284
Top 50

http://www.beanietop50.com
This is the biggest Beanie site-ranking list on the Web. All sites are ranked by the number of unique daily hits.

285
Heavy Graphics

http://www.angelfire.com/mo/AWOP/top50.html
Knipper says, "Knipper's Beanie Top 50 is a list of Beanie sites that provide valuable information, fair and reasonably priced Beanies & Beanie accessories for sale, contests, rumors and much more." Knipper is fond of graphics, so be patient while the site loads.

286
Top 20
http://beanietop20.hypermart.net/topsites/index.html
This "best of Beanies" site includes a few good ones to visit.

287
Planet Beanie
http://www.planetbeanie.com/topsites/vote.asp
Check it out, you might find some of these sites to be out of this world.

288
Fifty Something
http://jackandsasha.prohosting.com/top/topsites.html
Jack and Sasha have fifty Beanie sites for you to visit.

289
<u>Site Seeing</u>
http://www.encyclobeaniea.com/sitebeanies.htm
This Beanie compendium also has a lot of good sites.

290
<u>Addicted to Links</u>
http://www.addictedtobeaniebabies.com/links.html
Watch out for heavy graphics here. Click on any banner of interest.

291
<u>Links Galore</u>
http://www.whatsonthe.net/beaniemks.htm
3,500+ links. Happy surfing.

292
Buddy Links
http://www.beanie-buddy.com/blink.html
Lots of good links that are updated monthly.

293
Informative Links
http://www.beaniephiles.com/infolinks.html
This Beaniephile knows her stuff. While her links are not numerous, they are good.

294
Happy Links
http://happytoy.com/fusion/Links/links.htm
This site specializes in Teenie Beanies, and you will find many links related to them.

295
Let's Have Fun
http://www.funlist.com/www/ty
The Fun List has many Beanie sites. Totally unrelated to Beanies, it also has tons of information about another product people are passionate about—Coca-Cola.

296
Push Me to 'Em
http://www.plushcollector.com/links/links.html
This software vendor has lots of good links for you.

297
Tia's Awards
http://www.geocities.com/Heartland/Woods/2218/award.html
From Tia's award page, you'll be taken to many Beanie Web sites.

298
Clever Links
http://www.clever.net/chrisco/beanies/linx.htm
Here's a bunch of fan sites. See what others are doing, and maybe it will inspire you to create a Web site.

299
The Rascal House
http://home.att.net/~rascalz/blinks.html
This rascal categorizes his sites by recommended, personal and corporate.

300
Search the Net

http://www.momma.com
http://www.altavista.com
http://www.yahoo.com
http://www.hotbot.com
http://www.excite.com
http://www.lycos.com
http://www.askjeeves.com

There are certainly a few more Beanie sites that are worth visiting, so use these incredible search engines to find them. A recent search for "Beanie Babies" at Altavista netted over 75,000 sites. Enjoy your surfing.

INDEX (BY SITE NUMBER)

INDEX (BY SITE NUMBER)

The Incredible Newsletter

If you are enjoying this book, you can also arrange to receive a steady stream of more "incredible Internet things," delivered directly to your e-mail address.

The Leebow Letter, Ken Leebow's weekly e-mail newsletter, provides new sites, updates on existing ones and information about other happenings on the Internet.

For more details about *The Leebow Letter* and how to subscribe, send an e-mail to:

Newsletter@Mindspring.com